Oxford
International Primary
History

2

Helen Crawford

Oxford International Primary for enquiring minds

OXFORD
UNIVERSITY PRESS

Great Clarendon Street, Oxford, OX2 6DP, United Kingdom

Oxford University Press is a department of the University of Oxford. It furthers the University's objective of excellence in research, scholarship, and education by publishing worldwide. Oxford is a registered trade mark of Oxford University Press in the UK and in certain other countries.

British Library Cataloguing in Publication Data
Data available

ISBN 978-0-19-841810-8

7 9 10 8

Paper used in the production of this book is a natural, recyclable product made from wood grown in sustainable forests. The manufacturing process conforms to the environmental regulations of the country of origin.

Printed in India by Multivista Global Pvt. Ltd

Acknowledgements

Cover illustration: Carlos Molinari/Advocate Art

Artwork: Aptara

Photos: p4 (L), p16 & p46 (BR): Evikka/Shutterstock; **p4 (ML) & p16:** Mickey Mouse toy made by Dean's, English, 1930's (velvet)/Private Collection/Photo © Bonhams, London, UK/Bridgeman Images; **p2 (MR), p16 & p46 (BL):** DEA / A. DAGLI ORTI /Getty; **p4 (R) & p16:** INTERFOTO/Alamy; **p5 (L) & p16:** Science & Society Picture Library/Getty; **p5 (R) & p16:** Nieuwland Photography/Shutterstock; **p6:** Ruslan Guzov/Shutterstock; **p9 & p17 (L):** Interfoto/Mary Evans; **p10 (T) & p17 (M):** DEA/A. JEMOLO/Getty; **p10 (B) & p46 (BM):** Caroline P. Digonis/Alamy ; **p11:** Beepstock/Alamy; **p12 (T) & p46 (TR):** Rob Byron/Shutterstock; **p12 (BL) & p46 (TL):** Adrian Candela/Shutterstock; **p12 (BR):** Keystone-France/Getty; **p13:** INTERFOTO/TV-yesterday/Mary Evans; **p14:** Bettmann/Getty; **p14/15 & p17 (R):** DEA/A. DAGLI ORTI/Getty; **p15:** Stefano Ember/Shutterstock; **p18/19:** Ola_view/Shutterstock; **p18:** Everett - Art/Shutterstock; **p19 (L):** Everett Historical/Shutterstock; **p20 (R):** Tim Graham/Getty Images; **p21:** Queen Elizabeth I (1533-1603) being carried in Procession (Eliza Triumphans) c.1601 (oil on canvas), Peake, Robert (fl.1580-1626) (attr. to)/Private Collection/Bridgeman Images; **p22:** Princess Victoria (later Queen Victoria) aged nine, 1828 (panel), Smith, Stephen Catterson the Elder (1806-72)/Private Collection/© Christopher Wood Gallery, London, UK/Bridgeman Images; **p23:** John Frost Newspapers/Alamy; **p24:** Hulton Deutsch/Getty; **p25:** Tim Graham/Getty; **p26 (T) & p31 (L):** ACTIVE MUSEUM/Alamy Stock Photo; **p26 (B) & p31 (M):** GL Archive/Alamy; **p27 & p31 (R):** Tim Graham/Getty; **p32/33:** Wilbur Wright (1867-1912) in his 'flyer', before 1914 (colour litho), Pousthomis, Leon (1881-1916)/Musee de la Ville de Paris, Musee Carnavalet, Paris, France/Archives Charmet/Bridgeman Images; **p34 (T):** INTERFOTO / TV-yesterday/Mary Evans; **p34 (B) & p44 (L):** Mary Evans Picture Library; **p35 & p47 (L):** Mary Evans Picture Library; **p36, p44 (R) & p47 (ML):** Science & Society Picture Library/Getty; **p37 (L):** Steve Mann/Shutterstock; **p37 (R):** Steve Mann/Shutterstock; **p39 (T):** Fedor Selivanov/Shutterstock; **p39 (BL):** Everett Historical/Shutterstock; **p39 (BR):** boscorelli/Shutterstock; **p41:** SPUTNIK/Alamy; **p42:** Mike Collins, Neil Armstrong and Edwin Aldrin of Apollo 11 mission posing in front of their lunar landing module simulator at Cape Kennedy, Florida, 1969, photo NARA/Photo © Tallandier/Bridgeman Images; **p43 & p45:** Pictorial Press Ltd/Alamy;

Although we have made every effort to trace and contact all copyright holders before publication this has not been possible in all cases. If notified, the publisher will rectify any errors or omissions at the earliest opportunity.

Contents

1 Toys and games over time

In this unit you will:

- compare old and modern toys and games
- describe how toys and games have changed
- explain why toys and games have changed
- put toys and games in order on a timeline

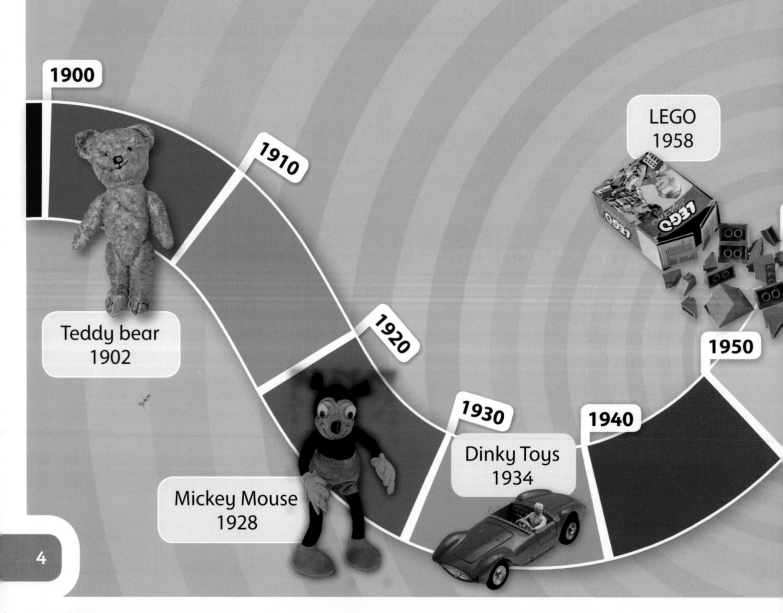

1900

1910

1920

1930

1940

1950

Teddy bear
1902

Mickey Mouse
1928

Dinky Toys
1934

LEGO
1958

Do you have a favourite toy or game? Children in the past also liked to play games. What did they play? What were their toys made of? How were their toys and games different from ours?

timeline
oral history
technology

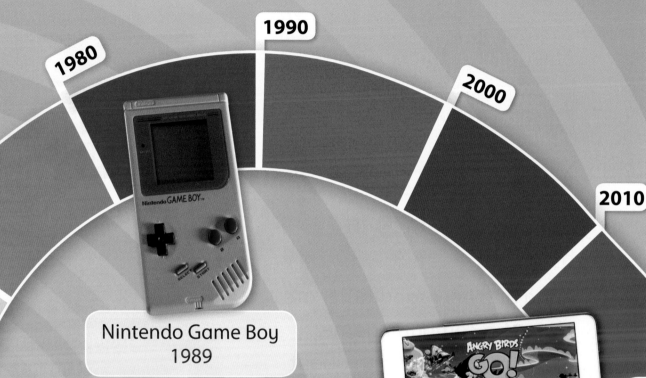

1980

1990

2000

1970

2010

Nintendo Game Boy
1989

Games on computer tablets
2010

? Look at the **timeline**. Which toys and games would you like to play with? Which is the oldest? Which is the newest? How do you know?

Some toys and games we play with today are very different from the toys and games children played with in the past. Some are very similar. Which toys and games are still popular today?

Sixty years ago computer games had not been invented. I played with different toys and games.

Toys and games in the past

Anna and her grandfather are playing a computer game. Grandfather tells Anna about the toys and games he played with when he was a boy.

I played chess with my friend.

I played with my toy cars.

> I also liked to fly my kite in the park.

Do you like to play with any of the toys that Anna's grandfather played with? Do you like to play any of the games he played?

What is oral history?

When people remember and talk about their life in the past, this is called **oral history**. Oral history is an important way to find out about the past.

Words

popular liked by many people

the past all the time before now

Activities

1 Write five questions to ask your grandparents about the toys and games they played with when they were young. Start your questions with 'What', 'Who', 'Where', 'When', 'How' or 'Why'.

2 Make a class display of the toys and games that your grandparents played with. Are any of these toys and games still popular today?

Challenge

Choose one game that your grandparents played. Talk to your grandparents and find out how this game has changed over time.

Teddy bears are popular toys all over the world. Why are they called 'teddy' bears? When were they first made? What were they made of?

How did the teddy bear get its name?

Teddy bears are named after Theodore Roosevelt. He was president of the USA from 1901 to 1909. His nickname was Teddy. One day, President Roosevelt went hunting with some friends. His friends caught a small bear for the president to shoot. He refused to shoot the bear because he had not caught it himself.

President Roosevelt refused to shoot a bear.

Word

modern from the time we live in now

The first teddy bears

The first teddy bears were made in 1902. They were handmade.

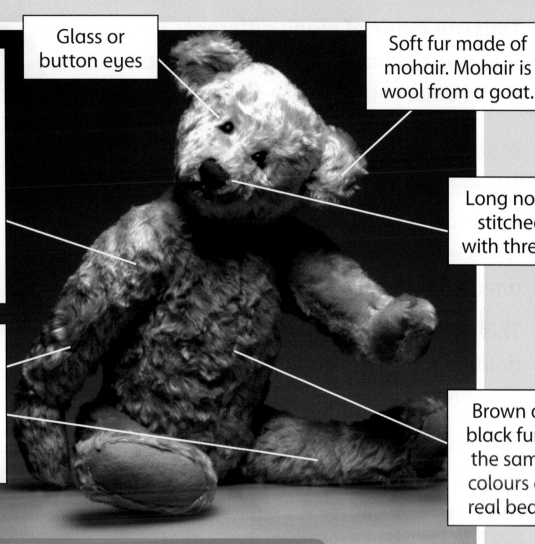

Glass or button eyes

Soft fur made of mohair. Mohair is wool from a goat.

The bear felt soft on the outside but was quite hard inside. It was filled with straw or very small pieces of wood.

Long nose, stitched with thread

The long arms and legs could move up, down and around.

Brown or black fur – the same colours as real bears

Activities

1 Look at a modern teddy bear.

   a Describe what you can see.

   b What is the teddy bear made of?

   c How does it feel?

2 Write three ways in which a modern teddy bear is different from the first teddy bears. Write three ways in which it is the same.

Challenge

Which bear is best to give to a baby: a modern bear or an old bear? Explain your ideas to a friend.

1.3 What were dolls made of?

Toys are made of many different materials. What materials were used to make dolls in the past?

Natural materials

The first dolls were made of natural materials such as wood, cloth or clay. Clay is wet earth that becomes hard when it is dried and heated.

This paddle doll is over 4000 years old. The doll is from Egypt. What materials is it made of?

A paddle doll

Some dolls were made using china. China is a type of clay that breaks easily.

This china doll was made in Germany 150 years ago. You can move the head, arms and legs of the doll.

Words

man-made made by people

material what something is made of

natural not made by people

A china doll

Man-made materials

From the 1950s, many dolls were made of plastic. Plastic is a man-made material. It is made in a factory using machines. Plastic is light and strong. It does not break easily.

Dolls' clothes

Dolls' clothes have changed over time because the clothes people wear have changed. Looking at dolls' clothes can tell us about the clothes that people wore in the past.

A modern plastic doll

Activities

1 Write a list of the different materials used to make dolls over time. Which material do you think is the best? Explain why.

2 Compare the clothes of the china doll with the clothes we wear today. Tell a friend your ideas.

Challenge

Draw a timeline showing how dolls' clothes have changed over time. Use the pictures on this page, reference books and the Internet to help you.

1.4 Making toys move

Toys that can move are great fun! People in the past used different ways to make moving toys. Changes in technology help us to invent new types of toys and games.

Puppets

A puppet is a model of a person or animal. The puppet in the photo is Mexican. It was made in about 1930. If you pull the strings you make the puppet move.

Strings

Clockwork toys

This is a toy robot from the 1950s. Inside the robot is a clockwork motor. You turn a key to wind up the motor and the robot begins to walk.

Key

Toys with electric motors

This doll was made in the 1960s. There is an electric motor inside the doll. You control the motor with a handset. A wire links the handset to the doll.

Handset

Wire

Computer games

In the 1970s, many people began to play games on a computer. You use a handset to make pictures on a screen move.

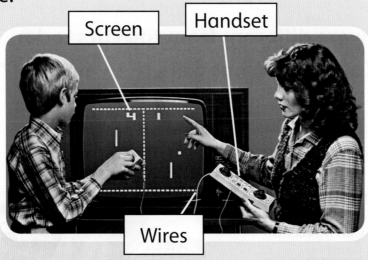

Screen

Handset

Wires

Activities

1 Think about the moving toys and games we play with today. How are they the same as the toys and games in the pictures? Tell a friend your ideas.

2 Draw a timeline.

   a Draw some toys on the timeline to show how moving toys have changed over time.

   b Add to the timeline one moving toy you play with today.

Challenge

Use reference books or the Internet to find out about other types of puppets from the past. How do we make these puppets move?

1.5 Why have toy cars changed?

The first toy cars were different from toy cars today. What did the first toy cars look like? What were they made of? How did they move?

Toy cars and real cars

Toy cars have changed over time because real cars have also changed. The cars we drive today look very different from the first cars.

One of Karl Benz's first cars

Did you know?

The first real car was invented in 1885 by Karl Benz.

Toy cars then and now

This toy car was made in the 1930s. The car is made of tin. How would you make this car move?

The modern toy car in the photo is made of plastic. How would you make this car move?

Some modern toy cars use an electric motor to move. The motor makes the car go fast, slow, forwards or backwards.

Activities

1 How is Karl Benz's car different from the cars people drive today? Tell a friend your ideas.

2 Make a fact file comparing old toy cars with modern toy cars. Think about:

   a what the cars look like

   b what the cars are made of

   c how the cars move.

Be a good historian

Good historians know there may be more than one reason why something changes over time. Why have toy cars changed? List all the reasons.

Challenge

Work together as a class. Find out three facts about Karl Benz and the first real car. For example, find answers to these questions: When was Karl Benz born? Where was he born? What was the name of the first car?

Answer these questions in your notebook.

Choose the best answer from the choices below. Write a, b or c as your answer.

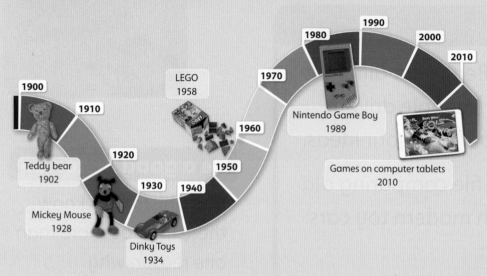

1 One game that was not played 60 years ago was:

  a chess

  b a computer game

  c kite flying

2 The teddy bear is named after an American:

  a president   b teacher   c sports star

3 The first dolls were made using natural materials such as:

  a wood, cloth, plastic

  b wood, clay, plastic

  c wood, cloth, clay

4 Computer games became popular in the:

  a 1930s   b 1950s   c 1970s

5   Old toy cars can tell us about:
    a   ships and trains
    b   what real cars looked like in the past
    c   roads in the past

Decide if these statements are true or false.
Write 'True' or 'False' for each one.

6   Some of the games we play today are the same as the games our grandparents played.

7   Plastic dolls are heavy and break easily.

8   We can make toys move using clockwork or electric motors.

Now answer these questions.

9   Why is oral history a good way to learn about the past? Write a sentence to explain your ideas.

10 Which toy do you think has changed the most over time – a teddy bear, a doll or a toy car? Write some sentences to explain your ideas.

2 Three English queens

In this unit you will:

- talk about the reigns of three English queens
- compare three different English queens
- compare life at different times in the past

A queen is a female ruler of a country. You are going to learn about three queens who have all ruled England. Who are they? When did they rule? Why are they special?

Queen Elizabeth I
1558–1603 CE

reign royal
empire
portrait

| 16th century | 17th century | 18th century |

? We use numbers called **Roman numerals** to show the order of kings or queens who have the same name.

The Roman numeral for 1 is **I**. Elizabeth **I** was the **first** Queen Elizabeth.

The Roman numeral for 2 is **II**. Elizabeth **II** is the **second** Queen Elizabeth.

Look at the numbers in the circles below. V = 5 and X = 10. Can you match the Roman numerals with the numbers 1–10?

X	II
V	VI	I
VIII	IX	III
IV	VII

1	2
3	4	5
6	7	8
9	10

Queen Victoria
1837–1901 CE

Queen Elizabeth II
1952–

| 19th century | 20th century | 21st century |

Elizabeth I was born in 1533 CE. She was very powerful and her reign as queen lasted 44 years. Elizabeth loved having fun, but she also faced danger.

Scotland
Ireland
England
Wales

Elizabeth the princess

Elizabeth grew up in a **royal** palace. Royal means something belonging to a king or queen. She did not go to school but she was clever and loved learning. She spoke many languages and could play musical instruments.

Elizabeth the queen

Elizabeth became queen in 1558. She did not get married, and ruled by herself. Elizabeth said she was 'married to England'.

Danger at sea!

In 1588, the king of Spain sent ships to attack England. The group of ships was called the Spanish Armada. Spanish and English ships fought a great battle at sea. England won the battle and Elizabeth was safe.

Word

armada a large group of ships

What is the royal court?

The royal court is all the people who live and work with a king or queen. Elizabeth and her royal court loved theatre and music. They travelled often, staying in palaces all around England.

Elizabeth's death

Elizabeth I's **reign** ended when she died in 1603. She had no children so her cousin, the King of Scotland, became the king. He was called James.

Activities

1 Elizabeth I said she was 'married to England'. What do you think she meant? Explain your ideas to a friend.

2 Look at the picture of Elizabeth I and the royal court. Talk to a friend about what you can see. Why do you think Elizabeth is being carried?

Challenge

Work together as a class. Find out why the Spanish king sent ships to attack England.

Victoria was queen for 63 years. During her long reign, she had both happy times and sad times. What was it like to live as queen for so long?

Victoria the princess

Victoria was born in 1819. She did not go to school. She had lessons at home. She was a lonely child and did not have many friends.

Victoria the queen

Victoria became queen in 1837 when she was 18 years old. She married her cousin Albert, who was from Germany. Victoria and Albert were very happy together and had nine children.

What was the British Empire?

An **empire** is a large number of countries ruled by one person. Victoria was ruler of the British Empire. The British Empire was the largest empire in history.

Did you know?

Victoria had more than 132 dolls.

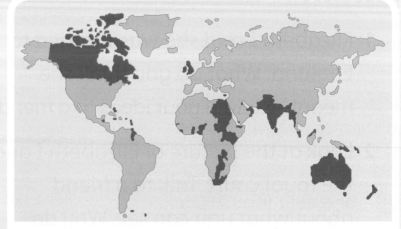

The countries in red were part of the British Empire during Queen Victoria's reign.

Sad times and happy times

In 1861, Albert died. Victoria was very sad. She wore black clothes as a sign of her sadness for the rest of her life.

In 1897, Victoria celebrated her Diamond Jubilee. This meant she had been queen for 60 years. She was the first king or queen of England to rule for such a long time.

Victoria's death

Victoria died in 1901. Her eldest son became King Edward VII.

Newspaper front page celebrating Queen Victoria's Diamond Jubilee

Activities

1 Draw a timeline from 1819 to 1901. Write on the timeline the events of Victoria's life.

2 Design your own newspaper front page to celebrate Victoria's Diamond Jubilee. Include a headline, a picture and two or three sentences about her long reign.

Word

event something important that happens

Challenge

Name three countries that were part of the British Empire. Use the map on page 22 and an atlas to help you. Choose one country from Asia, one from Africa and one from North or South America.

2.3 Who is Queen Elizabeth II?

Elizabeth II is queen of the United Kingdom (UK). As you read about Elizabeth II, think about how her reign is different from the reigns of Elizabeth I and Victoria. Think about how her reign is the same.

Elizabeth the princess

Elizabeth was born in 1926. She did not go to school. She had lessons at home. As a child, Elizabeth enjoyed playing outdoors. She loved horses.

Elizabeth the queen

In 1947, Elizabeth married Philip Mountbatten from Greece. They had four children.

In 1952, Elizabeth became queen. In the UK, 27 million people watched her coronation on television. This was the first time a royal coronation was shown on television.

During Elizabeth's reign the British Empire ended. The countries that were part of the British Empire became independent. This means that they ruled themselves.

On the move

Elizabeth II travels thousands of miles every year. She is the first English queen to fly in an airplane. She has visited more than 116 different countries.

Diamond Jubilee

In 2012, Elizabeth II celebrated her Diamond Jubilee. She had been queen for 60 years.

Word

coronation a ceremony when a person becomes king or queen

Activities

1 Write five questions you would like to ask Elizabeth II about her life as queen and how the world has changed during her reign.

2 Discuss in a group how the reign of Elizabeth II is the same as or different from the reigns of Elizabeth I and Victoria.

Challenge

Work together as a class. Choose one country Elizabeth II has visited. Find out about her royal visit. When did she visit? Who did she meet?

Did you know?

Queen Victoria was Elizabeth II's great-great-grandmother.

2.4 What can we learn from a portrait?

A portrait is a painting or photo of a person. Look at these portraits of Elizabeth I, Victoria and Elizabeth II. What do they tell us about each queen?

Queen Elizabeth I

This **portrait** was painted in 1592. The pearls are a symbol to show that she was not married. She is standing on the map to show she ruled England.

Queen Victoria

This portrait was painted in 1846.

Victoria is wearing a crown and sitting on a throne. This tells us she was a queen.

Victoria is with Albert and some of their children. This tells us Victoria was a wife and a mother.

Queen Elizabeth II

This portrait of Elizabeth II is not a painting. It is a photograph, taken in 1987.

Elizabeth is wearing a crown and standing in her royal palace to show she is a queen. Her jewels tell us she is rich.

Be a good historian

Good historians know that pictures can tell us about the past. Portraits tell us what people looked like and the clothes they wore. Portraits also tell us why some people in the past were important.

Word

symbol an object that represents something

Activities

1 Compare the portraits of the three queens. Tell a friend how they are similar and different from each other.

2 Draw a portrait of yourself. Show on your portrait the things that are important about you.

Challenge

Use the Internet to look at a portrait of another famous person from the past. Can you see any clues or symbols that give you more information about this person?

2.5 Different times

Elizabeth I, Victoria and Elizabeth II were queens at different times. Life was very different during each queen's reign. How did the world change when each queen ruled?

 ## Queen Elizabeth I

During Elizabeth I's reign, from 1558 to 1603, people learned new things about the world. The years of Elizabeth's reign were called the Golden Age in England.

Many people enjoyed music and the theatre. William Shakespeare wrote famous plays.

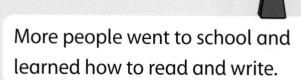

English ships sailed around the world for the first time.

More people went to school and learned how to read and write.

 ## Queen Victoria

During Victoria's reign, from 1837 to 1901, new inventions changed the world forever.

People travelled in steam trains.

Electric lights lit up streets and houses.

The telephone was invented.

Queen Elizabeth II

Since the beginning of Elizabeth II's reign in 1952, new technology has changed the world we live in.

Rockets travelled into space and some people went to the moon.

The mobile phone was invented.

The Internet connected computers all around the world.

Activities

1 Work in a group of three. Each of you is one of the queens you have learned about. Tell each other about all the changes that happened when you were queen.

2 Which queen, do you think, reigned in the most exciting time? Explain your ideas to a friend.

Challenge

Make a class display about each queen. Find out three facts about each queen. Find out three things that happened during each queen's reign. Add these to your display.

② Review

Answer these questions in your notebook.

Choose the best answer from the choices below.
Write a, b or c as your answer.

1 The Roman numeral for the number 5 is:

   a X   b III   c V

2 The people who live and work with a king or queen
are called the:

   a royal court

   b royal box

   c royal throne

3 When Elizabeth I was queen, the English were
attacked by:

   a French ships

   b Chinese ships

   c Spanish ships

4 A large number of countries ruled by one person
is called:

   a an empire   b an atlas   c a globe

5 The ceremony when someone becomes king or
queen is called a:

   a reign   b coronation   c party

Decide if these statements are true or false. Write 'True' or 'False' for each one.

6   Elizabeth I celebrated a diamond jubilee.

7   A portrait is a painting or photo that shows a person.

8   The telephone was invented during the reign of Queen Victoria.

Now answer these questions.

9   Why are portraits a good way to learn about people who lived in the past? Write a sentence to explain your ideas.

10 Which queen of England do you think was the most important: Elizabeth I, Victoria or Elizabeth II? Write one sentence about each queen.

3 Air and space travel

In this unit you will:

- describe how air travel developed over time
- compare old and modern airplanes
- discuss important events in the history of air and space travel

For thousands of years, people travelled by land and on water. Flying through the air was just a dream.

Today, airplanes fly all around the world and people have even been in rockets to the moon. When did air travel begin? Who invented the first **aircraft**? Who were the first people to go up, up and away?

? Look at this picture of an airplane. What can you see? How old do you think the airplane is? How is it different from the airplanes that fly in the sky today?

33

3.1 Up in a balloon

An aircraft is a machine that can fly through the air. What was the first aircraft? How did it fly? Who invented it?

A good idea!

Two brothers from France, Joseph and Étienne Montgolfier, had a good idea. They noticed that hot air rises. They wanted to use hot air to send a balloon up into the sky. They wanted to fly.

Animals in a balloon

The brothers made a large balloon from paper and cloth. They lit a fire under the balloon to make the air inside it hot. They put a duck, a rooster and a sheep in a basket. They attached the basket to the balloon.

In September 1793, hundreds of people watched the hot air balloon rise up into the sky.

The good idea had worked.

Flying with people

The brothers now wanted to test their aircraft by flying it with people as passengers. On 21 November 1783, they asked two men to fly in their balloon. The two men flew over the city of Paris. They flew for 25 minutes and travelled 10 kilometres.

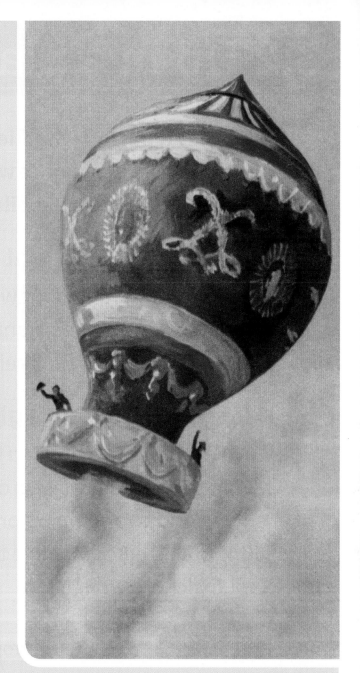

Activities

1 Why do you think the first balloon flight had animals as passengers instead of people? Explain your ideas to a friend.

2 Look at the picture of the two men in the balloon. Describe to a friend what you can see. Explain to your friend how the balloon flew in the sky.

Challenge

Abbas ibn Firnas lived in Spain 1200 years ago. He is an important person in the history of flight. Work together as a class to find out why.

3.2 Up in a plane

A pilot is a person who flies an aircraft. In 1903, the first airplane with an engine was built. Who invented it? How high did it fly? Who was the pilot?

Who were the Wright brothers?

Orville and Wilbur Wright were American brothers. They built bicycles but they wanted to build an airplane. They made kites to test their ideas.

The first airplane flight

The Wright brothers built a biplane. A biplane is an airplane that has two sets of wings. The biplane had an engine and two spinning propellers to give power. The **pilot** pulled wires to move the wings. This helped the biplane change direction.

The Wright brothers named their airplane 'Flyer'.

On 17 December 1903, the brothers were ready to test their biplane. They tossed a coin to decide who would fly. Orville was the pilot and Wilbur watched from the ground. The biplane flew for 12 seconds and went just 3 metres above the ground.

Stamps that celebrate the first airplane flight

The age of flying

The Wright brothers continued to build airplanes. Men and women trained to become pilots. They flew airplanes all over the world.

Lotfia El Nadi, from Egypt, became the first African woman pilot in 1933.

Word

toss a coin to decide between two choices by throwing a coin

Activities

1 Why do you think the Wright brothers made kites to test their ideas for an airplane? Explain your ideas to a friend.

2 Work with a partner. Imagine you are the Wright brothers. Make up a role play about what happened on 17 December 1903.

Challenge

Work together as a class to find out more about Lotfia El Nadi or another of the first women pilots.

Have you ever flown in an airplane? What was it like? How has air travel changed since the first airplane flights over a century ago?

Word

century one hundred years

How have airplanes changed over time?

Airplanes today are faster and safer than the first airplanes. They are powered by jet engines. Jet engines suck in air. The air burns with fuel to power the engine.

The Wright brothers' first plane flew just 3 metres above the ground. Modern airplanes can fly 12 000 metres above the ground. They are larger too. A modern airplane can fly with hundreds of passengers on board.

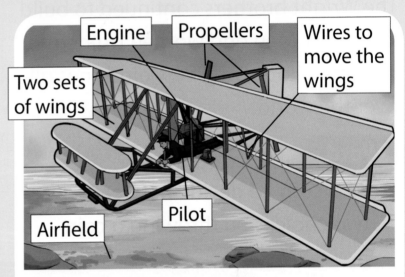

Engine   Propellers   Wires to move the wings

Two sets of wings

Pilot

Airfield

The Wright brothers' airplane – 1903

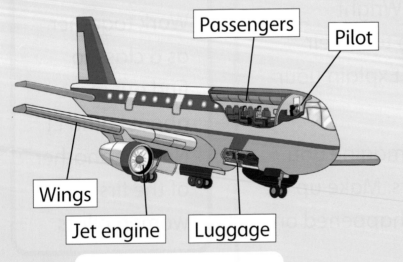

Passengers   Pilot

Wings

Jet engine   Luggage

A modern jet airplane

Be a good historian

Good historians compare the past with the world we live in today. This helps us understand what has changed over time and what has stayed the same.

At the airport

The first airplanes flew from airfields. Today most airplanes take off from and land at busy airports.

Most airports are named after places, but some airports are named after famous people.

More than 83 million passengers used Dubai International Airport in 2016.

Marco Polo airport in Venice, Italy, is named after a famous Italian explorer.

Challenge

Find three airports named after famous people. Who are these people? Why do we remember them?

Activities

1 Compare the picture of the modern jet airplane with the Wright brothers' airplane. Discuss with a friend how airplanes have changed over time and how they have stayed the same.

2 Make a fact file about your nearest airport.
   a What is the airport called?
   b When was it built?
   c How many places can you fly to from this airport?
   d Where can you fly to from this airport?

3.4 The Space Age

**An astronaut is a person who travels into space.
Who were the first astronauts? Where were they from?
When did their journey into space begin?**

What was the first space machine?

In October 1957, a machine called
Sputnik was sent into space.
Sputnik was a metal ball about the
size of a beach ball. It had four
transmitters that sent messages
back to Earth. A machine that
orbits Earth is called a satellite –
Sputnik was the first satellite.

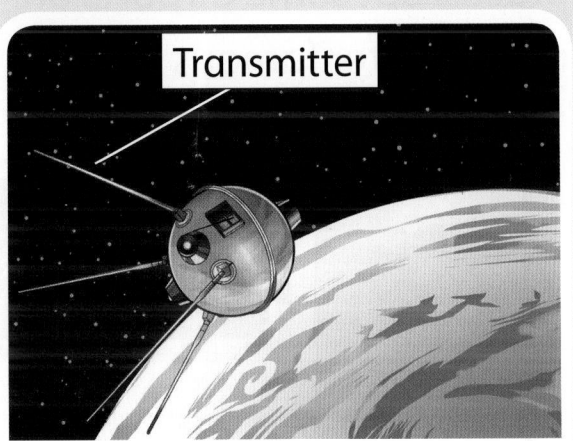

Transmitter

Sputnik orbited the Earth for
22 days.

A dog called Laika

In November 1957, a dog called
Laika was sent into space for
seven days. Laika proved that
animals could stay alive in space.

Who were the first astronauts?

In April 1961, a Russian
astronaut called Yuri Gagarin
became the first person to travel
into space. Gagarin's spacecraft
was called Vostok 1. Vostok 1
orbited the Earth for 108 minutes.

Yuri Gagarin

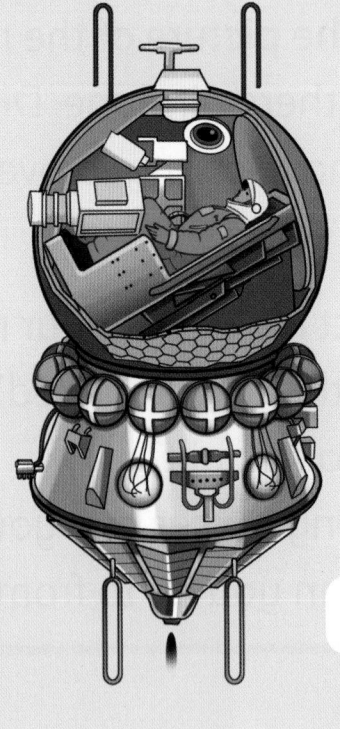

Vostok 1

Two years later, in 1963, Valentina Tereshkova became the first woman in space. She was also from Russia.

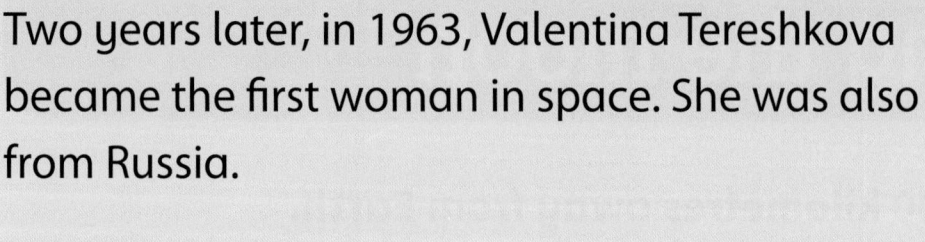

Walking in space

In March 1965, Alexey Leonov was the first astronaut to go on a spacewalk. He was connected to the spacecraft by a 5-metre cable. His spacewalk lasted for 12 minutes.

Valentina Tereshkova

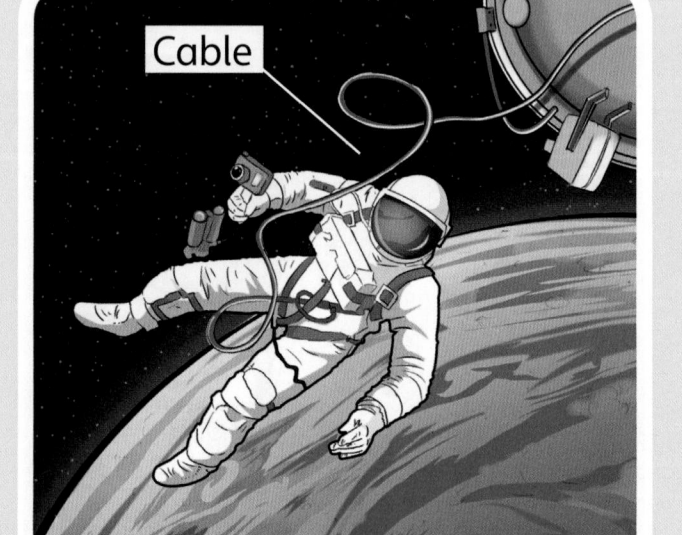

Cable

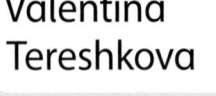

Words

orbit to go around a planet

spacewalk moving around in space, outside a spacecraft

Activities

1 Draw a timeline. Show on the timeline how space travel developed in the 1950s and 1960s.

2 Write five questions you would like to ask Yuri Gagarin about his journey into space.

Challenge

Russia was the first country to send an astronaut into space. Which country was the second? Which country was the third? Work together as a class to find out.

The moon is 384 400 kilometres away from Earth. How did astronauts reach the moon? When was the first moon landing? Who was the first person to walk on the moon?

Blast off!

On 16 July 1969, a US spacecraft called Apollo 11 went into space. Three astronauts were on board: Neil Armstrong, Edwin Aldrin and Michael Collins. Edwin Aldrin's nickname was Buzz.

Journey to the moon

The journey to the moon took five days. The astronauts ate food from plastic packets and they slept in sleeping bags. The sleeping bags were tied down because everything floats in space.

Michael Collins, Neil Armstrong and Buzz Aldrin

Moon landing

On 21 July 1969, Neil Armstrong and Buzz Aldrin landed on the moon. Michael Collins stayed in Apollo 11.

The moon landing was shown on television. Approximately 600 million people watched Neil Armstrong take the first steps on the moon.

Back to Earth

On 24 July 1969, Apollo 11 landed back on Earth. The astronauts brought back moon rocks that were 3.7 billion years old.

Did you know?

Neil Armstrong took a small piece of the Wright brothers' 1903 airplane to the moon. Why do you think he did this?

Neil Armstrong walked on the moon.

Activities

1 Neil Armstrong said: 'That's one small step for a man, one giant leap for mankind.' Explain to a friend what you think this means.

2 Work with a partner. One of you is a television reporter. One of you is an Apollo 11 astronaut. Make up a television interview about the moon landing.

Challenge

Use the Internet to watch television reports of the first moon landing. Describe what you can see to a friend.

Review

Answer these questions in your notebook.

Choose the best answer from the choices below.
Write a, b or c as your answer.

1   The first aircraft to fly in the air was:
   a   an airplane
   b   a hot air balloon
   c   a spacecraft

2   The first balloon flight took place in the:
   a   16th century
   b   18th century
   c   21st century

3   The first airplane with an engine was built by:
   a   the Montgolfier brothers
   b   the Armstrong brothers
   c   the Wright brothers

1783   1903

4 The first machine in space was called:

   a Apollo 11   **b** Vostok 1   **c** Sputnik

Decide if these statements are true or false. Write 'True' or 'False' for each one.

5 The first person to go into space was from Russia.

6 The first person to walk on the moon was called Yuri Gagarin.

7 Airplanes today are powered by jet engines.

Now complete these tasks.

8 Compare the first hot air balloon flight with the first airplane flight. Write about how the flights were different and how they were similar.

9 Who do you think was the bravest astronaut: Yuri Gagarin or Neil Armstrong? Write a paragraph to explain your ideas.

10 Look at the pictures. Which do you think is the most important event in the history of air travel? Write a paragraph to explain your ideas.

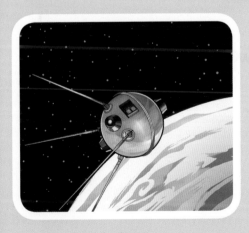

1957

1961

1969

Vocabulary quiz

Answer these questions in your notebook.

1 Toys and games over time

1 Match the words from the box with the pictures.

> car   doll   puppet   robot   teddy bear

a

b

c

d

e

2 Fill in the gaps using the words from the box.
  a Plastic is a ____ material.
  b Wood is a ____ ____.

> man-made   material   natural

2 Three English queens

1 Fill in the gaps using the words from the box.

  a Queen Elizabeth I's ____ lasted 44 years.

  b Queen Victoria ruled over a large ____.

  c Queen Elizabeth I grew up in a ____ palace.

> empire
> reign
> royal

2 Match the words from the box with the definitions.

  a a large group of ships

  b an object that represents something

  c a ceremony when a person becomes king or queen

> armada
> coronation
> symbol

3 The history of air travel

1 Match the words from the box with the definitions.

> aircraft   astronaut   pilot   orbit

  a to go around a planet

  b a person who flies an aircraft

  c a person who travels into space

  d a machine that can fly through the sky

2 What do these pictures show?
Choose the correct word from the box.

a  **b**  **c**  **d**  **e**

Glossary

aircraft a machine that can fly through the sky

armada a large group of ships

astronaut a person who travels into space

century one hundred years

coronation a ceremony when a person becomes king or queen

empire a large group of countries ruled by one person

event something important that happens

man-made made by people

material what something is made of

modern from the time we live in now

natural not made by people

oral history learning about the past from people who remember and talk about their life in the past

orbit to go around a planet

pilot a person who flies an aircraft

popular liked by many people

portrait a painting or photo of a person

reign the time when one king or queen rules

royal something belonging to a king or queen

spacewalk moving around in space, outside a spacecraft

symbol an object that represents something

technology using science to invent new things or to solve problems

the past all the time before now

timeline a way of showing events in order of when they happened, along a line

toss a coin to decide between two choices by throwing a coin